MYUSER/PASSWORDS

Little Acorn Books™

MY USER/PASSWORDS

For Your Internet Housekeeping

The perfect way to remember and keep your passwords secure.

AF798905

LAB201413P

Little Acorn Books™
is an imprint of

Little Acorn Associates, Inc.
Greensboro, NC
https://www.littleacornbooks.com

ISBN 978-1-937257-67-5
Printed in the United States of America

NOTES:

- **Web Address:** ____________________
User Name: ____________________
Passwords: ____________________

- **Web Address:** ____________________
User Name: ____________________
Passwords: ____________________

- **Web Address:** ____________________
User Name: ____________________
Passwords: ____________________

- **Web Address:** ____________________
User Name: ____________________
Passwords: ____________________

- **Web Address:** ____________________
User Name: ____________________
Passwords: ____________________

A

- **Web Address:** ______________________

User Name: ______________________

Passwords: ______________________

- **Web Address:** ______________________

User Name: ______________________

Passwords: ______________________

- **Web Address:** ______________________

User Name: ______________________

Passwords: ______________________

- **Web Address:** ______________________

User Name: ______________________

Passwords: ______________________

- **Web Address:** ______________________

User Name: ______________________

Passwords: ______________________

Keep this book in a safe place. Date and change your passwords periodically.

- Web Address:
User Name:
Passwords:

- Web Address:
User Name:
Passwords:

- Web Address:
User Name:
Passwords:

- Web Address:
User Name:
Passwords:

- Web Address:
User Name:
Passwords:

Keep this book in a safe place. Date and change your passwords periodically.

A

- **Web Address:** ______________________

User Name: ______________________

Passwords: ______________________

- **Web Address:** ______________________

User Name: ______________________

Passwords: ______________________

- **Web Address:** ______________________

User Name: ______________________

Passwords: ______________________

- **Web Address:** ______________________

User Name: ______________________

Passwords: ______________________

- **Web Address:** ______________________

User Name: ______________________

Passwords: ______________________

Keep this book in a safe place. Date and change your passwords periodically.

- **Web Address:**

User Name:

Passwords:

- **Web Address:**

User Name:

Passwords:

- **Web Address:**

User Name:

Passwords:

- **Web Address:**

User Name:

Passwords:

- **Web Address:**

User Name:

Passwords:

Keep this book in a safe place. Date and change your passwords periodically.

A

- **Web Address:** ____________________

User Name: ____________________

Passwords: ____________________

- **Web Address:** ____________________

User Name: ____________________

Passwords: ____________________

- **Web Address:** ____________________

User Name: ____________________

Passwords: ____________________

- **Web Address:** ____________________

User Name: ____________________

Passwords: ____________________

- **Web Address:** ____________________

User Name: ____________________

Passwords: ____________________

- **Web Address:** ____________________

User Name: ____________________

Passwords: ____________________

- **Web Address:** ____________________

User Name: ____________________

Passwords: ____________________

- **Web Address:** ____________________

User Name: ____________________

Passwords: ____________________

- **Web Address:** ____________________

User Name: ____________________

Passwords: ____________________

- **Web Address:** ____________________

User Name: ____________________

Passwords: ____________________

Keep this book in a safe place. Date and change your passwords periodically.

B

- **Web Address:** ______________________
User Name: ______________________
Passwords: ______________________

- **Web Address:** ______________________
User Name: ______________________
Passwords: ______________________

- **Web Address:** ______________________
User Name: ______________________
Passwords: ______________________

- **Web Address:** ______________________
User Name: ______________________
Passwords: ______________________

- **Web Address:** ______________________
User Name: ______________________
Passwords: ______________________

Keep this book in a safe place. Date and change your passwords periodically.

- Web Address:
User Name:
Passwords:

- Web Address:
User Name:
Passwords:

- Web Address:
User Name:
Passwords:

- Web Address:
User Name:
Passwords:

- Web Address:
User Name:
Passwords:

Keep this book in a safe place. Date and change your passwords periodically.

B

- Web Address:

User Name:

Passwords:

- Web Address:

User Name:

Passwords:

- Web Address:

User Name:

Passwords:

- Web Address:

User Name:

Passwords:

- Web Address:

User Name:

Passwords:

Keep this book in a safe place. Date and change your passwords periodically.

- Web Address:
User Name:
Passwords:

- Web Address:
User Name:
Passwords:

- Web Address:
User Name:
Passwords:

- Web Address:
User Name:
Passwords:

- Web Address:
User Name:
Passwords:

Keep this book in a safe place. Date and change your passwords periodically.

B

- **Web Address:** ______________________________
User Name: ______________________________
Passwords: ______________________________

- **Web Address:** ______________________________
User Name: ______________________________
Passwords: ______________________________

- **Web Address:** ______________________________
User Name: ______________________________
Passwords: ______________________________

- **Web Address:** ______________________________
User Name: ______________________________
Passwords: ______________________________

- **Web Address:** ______________________________
User Name: ______________________________
Passwords: ______________________________

- **Web Address:**
User Name:
Passwords:

- **Web Address:**
User Name:
Passwords:

- **Web Address:**
User Name:
Passwords:

- **Web Address:**
User Name:
Passwords:

- **Web Address:**
User Name:
Passwords:

Keep this book in a safe place. Date and change your passwords periodically.

C

- **Web Address:**

User Name:

Passwords:

- **Web Address:**

User Name:

Passwords:

- **Web Address:**

User Name:

Passwords:

- **Web Address:**

User Name:

Passwords:

- **Web Address:**

User Name:

Passwords:

- Web Address:
User Name:
Passwords:

- Web Address:
User Name:
Passwords:

- Web Address:
User Name:
Passwords:

- Web Address:
User Name:
Passwords:

- Web Address:
User Name:
Passwords:

Keep this book in a safe place. Date and change your passwords periodically.

C

- **Web Address:**

User Name:

Passwords:

- **Web Address:**

User Name:

Passwords:

- **Web Address:**

User Name:

Passwords:

- **Web Address:**

User Name:

Passwords:

- **Web Address:**

User Name:

Passwords:

Keep this book in a safe place. Date and change your passwords periodically.

- **Web Address:**

User Name:

Passwords:

- **Web Address:**

User Name:

Passwords:

- **Web Address:**

User Name:

Passwords:

- **Web Address:**

User Name:

Passwords:

- **Web Address:**

User Name:

Passwords:

Keep this book in a safe place. Date and change your passwords periodically.

C

- **Web Address:** ____________________
User Name: ____________________
Passwords: ____________________

- **Web Address:** ____________________
User Name: ____________________
Passwords: ____________________

- **Web Address:** ____________________
User Name: ____________________
Passwords: ____________________

- **Web Address:** ____________________
User Name: ____________________
Passwords: ____________________

- **Web Address:** ____________________
User Name: ____________________
Passwords: ____________________

- Web Address:

User Name:

Passwords:

- Web Address:

User Name:

Passwords:

- Web Address:

User Name:

Passwords:

- Web Address:

User Name:

Passwords:

- Web Address:

User Name:

Passwords:

Keep this book in a safe place. Date and change your passwords periodically.

D

- **Web Address:**

User Name:

Passwords:

- **Web Address:**

User Name:

Passwords:

- **Web Address:**

User Name:

Passwords:

- **Web Address:**

User Name:

Passwords:

- **Web Address:**

User Name:

Passwords:

- Web Address:

User Name:

Passwords:

- Web Address:

User Name:

Passwords:

- Web Address:

User Name:

Passwords:

- Web Address:

User Name:

Passwords:

- Web Address:

User Name:

Passwords:

D

- **Web Address:**

User Name:

Passwords:

- **Web Address:**

User Name:

Passwords:

- **Web Address:**

User Name:

Passwords:

- **Web Address:**

User Name:

Passwords:

- **Web Address:**

User Name:

Passwords:

Keep this book in a safe place. Date and change your passwords periodically.

- **Web Address:** ______________________________

User Name: ______________________________

Passwords: ______________________________

- **Web Address:** ______________________________

User Name: ______________________________

Passwords: ______________________________

- **Web Address:** ______________________________

User Name: ______________________________

Passwords: ______________________________

- **Web Address:** ______________________________

User Name: ______________________________

Passwords: ______________________________

- **Web Address:** ______________________________

User Name: ______________________________

Passwords: ______________________________

D

- **Web Address:** ____________________

User Name: ____________________

Passwords: ____________________

- **Web Address:** ____________________

User Name: ____________________

Passwords: ____________________

- **Web Address:** ____________________

User Name: ____________________

Passwords: ____________________

- **Web Address:** ____________________

User Name: ____________________

Passwords: ____________________

- **Web Address:** ____________________

User Name: ____________________

Passwords: ____________________

Keep this book in a safe place. Date and change your passwords periodically.

- Web Address:
User Name:
Passwords:

- Web Address:
User Name:
Passwords:

- Web Address:
User Name:
Passwords:

- Web Address:
User Name:
Passwords:

- Web Address:
User Name:
Passwords:

Keep this book in a safe place. Date and change your passwords periodically.

E

- Web Address:

User Name:

Passwords:

- Web Address:

User Name:

Passwords:

- Web Address:

User Name:

Passwords:

- Web Address:

User Name:

Passwords:

- Web Address:

User Name:

Passwords:

Keep this book in a safe place. Date and change your passwords periodically.

• Web Address: ____________________
User Name: ____________________
Passwords: ____________________

• Web Address: ____________________
User Name: ____________________
Passwords: ____________________

• Web Address: ____________________
User Name: ____________________
Passwords: ____________________

• Web Address: ____________________
User Name: ____________________
Passwords: ____________________

• Web Address: ____________________
User Name: ____________________
Passwords: ____________________

Keep this book in a safe place. Date and change your passwords periodically.

E

- Web Address: ___
User Name: ___
Passwords: ___

- Web Address: ___
User Name: ___
Passwords: ___

- Web Address: ___
User Name: ___
Passwords: ___

- Web Address: ___
User Name: ___
Passwords: ___

- Web Address: ___
User Name: ___
Passwords: ___

Keep this book in a safe place. Date and change your passwords periodically.

- Web Address:
User Name:
Passwords:

- Web Address:
User Name:
Passwords:

- Web Address:
User Name:
Passwords:

- Web Address:
User Name:
Passwords:

- Web Address:
User Name:
Passwords:

Keep this book in a safe place. Date and change your passwords periodically.

E

- **Web Address:**

User Name:

Passwords:

- **Web Address:**

User Name:

Passwords:

- **Web Address:**

User Name:

Passwords:

- **Web Address:**

User Name:

Passwords:

- **Web Address:**

User Name:

Passwords:

Keep this book in a safe place. Date and change your passwords periodically.

- **Web Address:**

User Name:

Passwords:

- **Web Address:**

User Name:

Passwords:

- **Web Address:**

User Name:

Passwords:

- **Web Address:**

User Name:

Passwords:

- **Web Address:**

User Name:

Passwords:

Keep this book in a safe place. Date and change your passwords periodically.

F

- **Web Address:**

User Name:

Passwords:

- **Web Address:**

User Name:

Passwords:

- **Web Address:**

User Name:

Passwords:

- **Web Address:**

User Name:

Passwords:

- **Web Address:**

User Name:

Passwords:

- Web Address:
User Name:
Passwords:

- Web Address:
User Name:
Passwords:

- Web Address:
User Name:
Passwords:

- Web Address:
User Name:
Passwords:

- Web Address:
User Name:
Passwords:

Keep this book in a safe place. Date and change your passwords periodically.

F

- **Web Address:** ___________________________

User Name: ___________________________

Passwords: ___________________________

- **Web Address:** ___________________________

User Name: ___________________________

Passwords: ___________________________

- **Web Address:** ___________________________

User Name: ___________________________

Passwords: ___________________________

- **Web Address:** ___________________________

User Name: ___________________________

Passwords: ___________________________

- **Web Address:** ___________________________

User Name: ___________________________

Passwords: ___________________________

Keep this book in a safe place. Date and change your passwords periodically.

- Web Address:
User Name:
Passwords:

- Web Address:
User Name:
Passwords:

- Web Address:
User Name:
Passwords:

- Web Address:
User Name:
Passwords:

- Web Address:
User Name:
Passwords:

Keep this book in a safe place. Date and change your passwords periodically.

F

- **Web Address:**
User Name:
Passwords:

- **Web Address:**
User Name:
Passwords:

- **Web Address:**
User Name:
Passwords:

- **Web Address:**
User Name:
Passwords:

- **Web Address:**
User Name:
Passwords:

- Web Address:

User Name:

Passwords:

- Web Address:

User Name:

Passwords:

- Web Address:

User Name:

Passwords:

- Web Address:

User Name:

Passwords:

- Web Address:

User Name:

Passwords:

G

- Web Address:

User Name:

Passwords:

- Web Address:

User Name:

Passwords:

- Web Address:

User Name:

Passwords:

- Web Address:

User Name:

Passwords:

- Web Address:

User Name:

Passwords:

- Web Address:

User Name:

Passwords:

- Web Address:

User Name:

Passwords:

- Web Address:

User Name:

Passwords:

- Web Address:

User Name:

Passwords:

- Web Address:

User Name:

Passwords:

G

- Web Address:

User Name:

Passwords:

- Web Address:

User Name:

Passwords:

- Web Address:

User Name:

Passwords:

- Web Address:

User Name:

Passwords:

- Web Address:

User Name:

Passwords:

Keep this book in a safe place. Date and change your passwords periodically.

- Web Address:
User Name:
Passwords:

- Web Address:
User Name:
Passwords:

- Web Address:
User Name:
Passwords:

- Web Address:
User Name:
Passwords:

- Web Address:
User Name:
Passwords:

G

- **Web Address:**

User Name:
Passwords:

- **Web Address:**

User Name:
Passwords:

- **Web Address:**

User Name:
Passwords:

- **Web Address:**

User Name:
Passwords:

- **Web Address:**

User Name:
Passwords:

Keep this book in a safe place. Date and change your passwords periodically.

- **Web Address:**

User Name:

Passwords:

- **Web Address:**

User Name:

Passwords:

- **Web Address:**

User Name:

Passwords:

- **Web Address:**

User Name:

Passwords:

- **Web Address:**

User Name:

Passwords:

H

- Web Address:

User Name:

Passwords:

- Web Address:

User Name:

Passwords:

- Web Address:

User Name:

Passwords:

- Web Address:

User Name:

Passwords:

- Web Address:

User Name:

Passwords:

- Web Address:

User Name:

Passwords:

- Web Address:

User Name:

Passwords:

- Web Address:

User Name:

Passwords:

- Web Address:

User Name:

Passwords:

- Web Address:

User Name:

Passwords:

Keep this book in a safe place. Date and change your passwords periodically.

H

- Web Address:

User Name:

Passwords:

- Web Address:

User Name:

Passwords:

- Web Address:

User Name:

Passwords:

- Web Address:

User Name:

Passwords:

- Web Address:

User Name:

Passwords:

Keep this book in a safe place. Date and change your passwords periodically.

- Web Address:

User Name:

Passwords:

- Web Address:

User Name:

Passwords:

- Web Address:

User Name:

Passwords:

- Web Address:

User Name:

Passwords:

- Web Address:

User Name:

Passwords:

Keep this book in a safe place. Date and change your passwords periodically.

H

- **Web Address:** ______________________________

User Name: ______________________________

Passwords: ______________________________

- **Web Address:** ______________________________

User Name: ______________________________

Passwords: ______________________________

- **Web Address:** ______________________________

User Name: ______________________________

Passwords: ______________________________

- **Web Address:** ______________________________

User Name: ______________________________

Passwords: ______________________________

- **Web Address:** ______________________________

User Name: ______________________________

Passwords: ______________________________

- Web Address:

User Name:

Passwords:

- Web Address:

User Name:

Passwords:

- Web Address:

User Name:

Passwords:

- Web Address:

User Name:

Passwords:

- Web Address:

User Name:

Passwords:

Keep this book in a safe place. Date and change your passwords periodically.

- Web Address:
User Name:
Passwords:

- Web Address:
User Name:
Passwords:

- Web Address:
User Name:
Passwords:

- Web Address:
User Name:
Passwords:

- Web Address:
User Name:
Passwords:

Keep this book in a safe place. Date and change your passwords periodically.

- **Web Address:** ____________________
User Name: ____________________
Passwords: ____________________

- **Web Address:** ____________________
User Name: ____________________
Passwords: ____________________

- **Web Address:** ____________________
User Name: ____________________
Passwords: ____________________

- **Web Address:** ____________________
User Name: ____________________
Passwords: ____________________

- **Web Address:** ____________________
User Name: ____________________
Passwords: ____________________

I

- **Web Address:**

User Name:

Passwords:

- **Web Address:**

User Name:

Passwords:

- **Web Address:**

User Name:

Passwords:

- **Web Address:**

User Name:

Passwords:

- **Web Address:**

User Name:

Passwords:

- Web Address:

User Name:

Passwords:

- Web Address:

User Name:

Passwords:

- Web Address:

User Name:

Passwords:

- Web Address:

User Name:

Passwords:

- Web Address:

User Name:

Passwords:

Keep this book in a safe place. Date and change your passwords periodically.

I

- **Web Address:** ____________________
User Name: ____________________
Passwords: ____________________

- **Web Address:** ____________________
User Name: ____________________
Passwords: ____________________

- **Web Address:** ____________________
User Name: ____________________
Passwords: ____________________

- **Web Address:** ____________________
User Name: ____________________
Passwords: ____________________

- **Web Address:** ____________________
User Name: ____________________
Passwords: ____________________

Keep this book in a safe place. Date and change your passwords periodically.

- Web Address:

User Name:

Passwords:

- Web Address:

User Name:

Passwords:

- Web Address:

User Name:

Passwords:

- Web Address:

User Name:

Passwords:

- Web Address:

User Name:

Passwords:

Keep this book in a safe place. Date and change your passwords periodically.

J

- **Web Address:**

User Name:

Passwords:

- **Web Address:**

User Name:

Passwords:

- **Web Address:**

User Name:

Passwords:

- **Web Address:**

User Name:

Passwords:

- **Web Address:**

User Name:

Passwords:

Keep this book in a safe place. Date and change your passwords periodically.

- **Web Address:**
User Name:
Passwords:

- **Web Address:**
User Name:
Passwords:

- **Web Address:**
User Name:
Passwords:

- **Web Address:**
User Name:
Passwords:

- **Web Address:**
User Name:
Passwords:

Keep this book in a safe place. Date and change your passwords periodically.

J

- **Web Address:**

User Name:

Passwords:

- **Web Address:**

User Name:

Passwords:

- **Web Address:**

User Name:

Passwords:

- **Web Address:**

User Name:

Passwords:

- **Web Address:**

User Name:

Passwords:

- Web Address:
User Name:
Passwords:

- Web Address:
User Name:
Passwords:

- Web Address:
User Name:
Passwords:

- Web Address:
User Name:
Passwords:

- Web Address:
User Name:
Passwords:

Keep this book in a safe place. Date and change your passwords periodically.

J

- **Web Address:**

User Name:

Passwords:

- **Web Address:**

User Name:

Passwords:

- **Web Address:**

User Name:

Passwords:

- **Web Address:**

User Name:

Passwords:

- **Web Address:**

User Name:

Passwords:

- Web Address:

User Name:

Passwords:

- Web Address:

User Name:

Passwords:

- Web Address:

User Name:

Passwords:

- Web Address:

User Name:

Passwords:

- Web Address:

User Name:

Passwords:

Keep this book in a safe place. Date and change your passwords periodically.

K

- Web Address:
User Name:
Passwords:

- Web Address:
User Name:
Passwords:

- Web Address:
User Name:
Passwords:

- Web Address:
User Name:
Passwords:

- Web Address:
User Name:
Passwords:

- **Web Address:** ______________________
User Name: ______________________
Passwords: ______________________

- **Web Address:** ______________________
User Name: ______________________
Passwords: ______________________

- **Web Address:** ______________________
User Name: ______________________
Passwords: ______________________

- **Web Address:** ______________________
User Name: ______________________
Passwords: ______________________

- **Web Address:** ______________________
User Name: ______________________
Passwords: ______________________

K

- Web Address:

User Name:

Passwords:

- Web Address:

User Name:

Passwords:

- Web Address:

User Name:

Passwords:

- Web Address:

User Name:

Passwords:

- Web Address:

User Name:

Passwords:

Keep this book in a safe place. Date and change your passwords periodically.

- Web Address:

User Name:

Passwords:

- Web Address:

User Name:

Passwords:

- Web Address:

User Name:

Passwords:

- Web Address:

User Name:

Passwords:

- Web Address:

User Name:

Passwords:

Keep this book in a safe place. Date and change your passwords periodically.

K

- **Web Address:** ____________________
User Name: ____________________
Passwords: ____________________

- **Web Address:** ____________________
User Name: ____________________
Passwords: ____________________

- **Web Address:** ____________________
User Name: ____________________
Passwords: ____________________

- **Web Address:** ____________________
User Name: ____________________
Passwords: ____________________

- **Web Address:** ____________________
User Name: ____________________
Passwords: ____________________

- Web Address:

User Name:

Passwords:

- Web Address:

User Name:

Passwords:

- Web Address:

User Name:

Passwords:

- Web Address:

User Name:

Passwords:

- Web Address:

User Name:

Passwords:

Keep this book in a safe place. Date and change your passwords periodically.

L

- **Web Address:**

User Name:

Passwords:

- **Web Address:**

User Name:

Passwords:

- **Web Address:**

User Name:

Passwords:

- **Web Address:**

User Name:

Passwords:

- **Web Address:**

User Name:

Passwords:

- Web Address:
User Name:
Passwords:

- Web Address:
User Name:
Passwords:

- Web Address:
User Name:
Passwords:

- Web Address:
User Name:
Passwords:

- Web Address:
User Name:
Passwords:

Keep this book in a safe place. Date and change your passwords periodically.

L

- **Web Address:**

User Name:

Passwords:

- **Web Address:**

User Name:

Passwords:

- **Web Address:**

User Name:

Passwords:

- **Web Address:**

User Name:

Passwords:

- **Web Address:**

User Name:

Passwords:

- Web Address:
User Name:
Passwords:

- Web Address:
User Name:
Passwords:

- Web Address:
User Name:
Passwords:

- Web Address:
User Name:
Passwords:

- Web Address:
User Name:
Passwords:

Keep this book in a safe place. Date and change your passwords periodically.

L

- **Web Address:** ___
User Name: ___
Passwords: ___

- **Web Address:** ___
User Name: ___
Passwords: ___

- **Web Address:** ___
User Name: ___
Passwords: ___

- **Web Address:** ___
User Name: ___
Passwords: ___

- **Web Address:** ___
User Name: ___
Passwords: ___

- Web Address:
User Name:
Passwords:

- Web Address:
User Name:
Passwords:

- Web Address:
User Name:
Passwords:

- Web Address:
User Name:
Passwords:

- Web Address:
User Name:
Passwords:

Keep this book in a safe place. Date and change your passwords periodically.

M

- **Web Address:**

User Name:

Passwords:

- **Web Address:**

User Name:

Passwords:

- **Web Address:**

User Name:

Passwords:

- **Web Address:**

User Name:

Passwords:

- **Web Address:**

User Name:

Passwords:

- Web Address:
User Name:
Passwords:

- Web Address:
User Name:
Passwords:

- Web Address:
User Name:
Passwords:

- Web Address:
User Name:
Passwords:

- Web Address:
User Name:
Passwords:

Keep this book in a safe place. Date and change your passwords periodically.

M

- **Web Address:** ______________________

User Name: ______________________

Passwords: ______________________

- **Web Address:** ______________________

User Name: ______________________

Passwords: ______________________

- **Web Address:** ______________________

User Name: ______________________

Passwords: ______________________

- **Web Address:** ______________________

User Name: ______________________

Passwords: ______________________

- **Web Address:** ______________________

User Name: ______________________

Passwords: ______________________

- Web Address:
User Name:
Passwords:

- Web Address:
User Name:
Passwords:

- Web Address:
User Name:
Passwords:

- Web Address:
User Name:
Passwords:

- Web Address:
User Name:
Passwords:

Keep this book in a safe place. Date and change your passwords periodically.

M

- **Web Address:**
User Name:
Passwords:

- **Web Address:**
User Name:
Passwords:

- **Web Address:**
User Name:
Passwords:

- **Web Address:**
User Name:
Passwords:

- **Web Address:**
User Name:
Passwords:

- Web Address:
User Name:
Passwords:

- Web Address:
User Name:
Passwords:

- Web Address:
User Name:
Passwords:

- Web Address:
User Name:
Passwords:

- Web Address:
User Name:
Passwords:

N

- Web Address:
User Name:
Passwords:

- Web Address:
User Name:
Passwords:

- Web Address:
User Name:
Passwords:

- Web Address:
User Name:
Passwords:

- Web Address:
User Name:
Passwords:

Keep this book in a safe place. Date and change your passwords periodically.

- Web Address:
User Name:
Passwords:

- Web Address:
User Name:
Passwords:

- Web Address:
User Name:
Passwords:

- Web Address:
User Name:
Passwords:

- Web Address:
User Name:
Passwords:

Keep this book in a safe place. Date and change your passwords periodically.

N

- Web Address: ______

User Name: ______
Passwords: ______

- Web Address: ______

User Name: ______
Passwords: ______

- Web Address: ______

User Name: ______
Passwords: ______

- Web Address: ______

User Name: ______
Passwords: ______

- Web Address: ______

User Name: ______
Passwords: ______

Keep this book in a safe place. Date and change your passwords periodically.

- Web Address:

User Name:

Passwords:

- Web Address:

User Name:

Passwords:

- Web Address:

User Name:

Passwords:

- Web Address:

User Name:

Passwords:

- Web Address:

User Name:

Passwords:

Keep this book in a safe place. Date and change your passwords periodically.

N

- **Web Address:** ______________________
User Name: ______________________
Passwords: ______________________

- **Web Address:** ______________________
User Name: ______________________
Passwords: ______________________

- **Web Address:** ______________________
User Name: ______________________
Passwords: ______________________

- **Web Address:** ______________________
User Name: ______________________
Passwords: ______________________

- **Web Address:** ______________________
User Name: ______________________
Passwords: ______________________

- Web Address:

User Name:

Passwords:

- Web Address:

User Name:

Passwords:

- Web Address:

User Name:

Passwords:

- Web Address:

User Name:

Passwords:

- Web Address:

User Name:

Passwords:

Keep this book in a safe place. Date and change your passwords periodically.

O

- **Web Address:** __________
User Name: __________
Passwords: __________

- **Web Address:** __________
User Name: __________
Passwords: __________

- **Web Address:** __________
User Name: __________
Passwords: __________

- **Web Address:** __________
User Name: __________
Passwords: __________

- **Web Address:** __________
User Name: __________
Passwords: __________

- **Web Address:**

User Name:
Passwords:

- **Web Address:**

User Name:
Passwords:

- **Web Address:**

User Name:
Passwords:

- **Web Address:**

User Name:
Passwords:

- **Web Address:**

User Name:
Passwords:

Keep this book in a safe place. Date and change your passwords periodically.

O

- Web Address: ______________________
User Name: ______________________
Passwords: ______________________

- Web Address: ______________________
User Name: ______________________
Passwords: ______________________

- Web Address: ______________________
User Name: ______________________
Passwords: ______________________

- Web Address: ______________________
User Name: ______________________
Passwords: ______________________

- Web Address: ______________________
User Name: ______________________
Passwords: ______________________

Keep this book in a safe place. Date and change your passwords periodically.

- Web Address: ______________________

User Name: ______________________

Passwords: ______________________

- Web Address: ______________________

User Name: ______________________

Passwords: ______________________

- Web Address: ______________________

User Name: ______________________

Passwords: ______________________

- Web Address: ______________________

User Name: ______________________

Passwords: ______________________

- Web Address: ______________________

User Name: ______________________

Passwords: ______________________

Keep this book in a safe place. Date and change your passwords periodically.

O

- **Web Address:** ______________________________

User Name: ______________________________

Passwords: ______________________________

____

____

____

____

- **Web Address:** ______________________________

User Name: ______________________________

Passwords: ______________________________

____

____

____

____

- **Web Address:** ______________________________

User Name: ______________________________

Passwords: ______________________________

____

____

____

____

- **Web Address:** ______________________________

User Name: ______________________________

Passwords: ______________________________

____

____

____

____

- **Web Address:** ______________________________

User Name: ______________________________

Passwords: ______________________________

____

____

____

____

- Web Address:
User Name:
Passwords:

- Web Address:
User Name:
Passwords:

- Web Address:
User Name:
Passwords:

- Web Address:
User Name:
Passwords:

- Web Address:
User Name:
Passwords:

Keep this book in a safe place. Date and change your passwords periodically.

P

- Web Address: ______
User Name: ______
Passwords: ______

- Web Address: ______
User Name: ______
Passwords: ______

- Web Address: ______
User Name: ______
Passwords: ______

- Web Address: ______
User Name: ______
Passwords: ______

- Web Address: ______
User Name: ______
Passwords: ______

Keep this book in a safe place. Date and change your passwords periodically.

- **Web Address:** ____________________
User Name: ____________________
Passwords: ____________________

- **Web Address:** ____________________
User Name: ____________________
Passwords: ____________________

- **Web Address:** ____________________
User Name: ____________________
Passwords: ____________________

- **Web Address:** ____________________
User Name: ____________________
Passwords: ____________________

- **Web Address:** ____________________
User Name: ____________________
Passwords: ____________________

P

- **Web Address:** ______

User Name: ______

Passwords: ______

- **Web Address:** ______

User Name: ______

Passwords: ______

- **Web Address:** ______

User Name: ______

Passwords: ______

- **Web Address:** ______

User Name: ______

Passwords: ______

- **Web Address:** ______

User Name: ______

Passwords: ______

Keep this book in a safe place. Date and change your passwords periodically.

- Web Address:

User Name:

Passwords:

- Web Address:

User Name:

Passwords:

- Web Address:

User Name:

Passwords:

- Web Address:

User Name:

Passwords:

- Web Address:

User Name:

Passwords:

Keep this book in a safe place. Date and change your passwords periodically.

P

- **Web Address:** ____________________

User Name: ____________________

Passwords: ____________________

- **Web Address:** ____________________

User Name: ____________________

Passwords: ____________________

- **Web Address:** ____________________

User Name: ____________________

Passwords: ____________________

- **Web Address:** ____________________

User Name: ____________________

Passwords: ____________________

- **Web Address:** ____________________

User Name: ____________________

Passwords: ____________________

- Web Address:

User Name:

Passwords:

- Web Address:

User Name:

Passwords:

- Web Address:

User Name:

Passwords:

- Web Address:

User Name:

Passwords:

- Web Address:

User Name:

Passwords:

Keep this book in a safe place. Date and change your passwords periodically.

Q

- Web Address:
User Name:
Passwords:

- Web Address:
User Name:
Passwords:

- Web Address:
User Name:
Passwords:

- Web Address:
User Name:
Passwords:

- Web Address:
User Name:
Passwords:

Keep this book in a safe place. Date and change your passwords periodically.

Q

- **Web Address:**

User Name:

Passwords:

- **Web Address:**

User Name:

Passwords:

- **Web Address:**

User Name:

Passwords:

- **Web Address:**

User Name:

Passwords:

- **Web Address:**

User Name:

Passwords:

Keep this book in a safe place. Date and change your passwords periodically.

Q

- **Web Address:** ______________________

User Name: ______________________

Passwords: ______________________

- **Web Address:** ______________________

User Name: ______________________

Passwords: ______________________

- **Web Address:** ______________________

User Name: ______________________

Passwords: ______________________

- **Web Address:** ______________________

User Name: ______________________

Passwords: ______________________

- **Web Address:** ______________________

User Name: ______________________

Passwords: ______________________

Keep this book in a safe place. Date and change your passwords periodically.

- Web Address:

User Name:

Passwords:

- Web Address:

User Name:

Passwords:

- Web Address:

User Name:

Passwords:

- Web Address:

User Name:

Passwords:

- Web Address:

User Name:

Passwords:

Keep this book in a safe place. Date and change your passwords periodically.

Q

- **Web Address:** ____________________

User Name: ____________________

Passwords: ____________________

- **Web Address:** ____________________

User Name: ____________________

Passwords: ____________________

- **Web Address:** ____________________

User Name: ____________________

Passwords: ____________________

- **Web Address:** ____________________

User Name: ____________________

Passwords: ____________________

- **Web Address:** ____________________

User Name: ____________________

Passwords: ____________________

Keep this book in a safe place. Date and change your passwords periodically.

- Web Address:
User Name:
Passwords:

- Web Address:
User Name:
Passwords:

- Web Address:
User Name:
Passwords:

- Web Address:
User Name:
Passwords:

- Web Address:
User Name:
Passwords:

Keep this book in a safe place. Date and change your passwords periodically.

R

- Web Address:

User Name:

Passwords:

- Web Address:

User Name:

Passwords:

- Web Address:

User Name:

Passwords:

- Web Address:

User Name:

Passwords:

- Web Address:

User Name:

Passwords:

Keep this book in a safe place. Date and change your passwords periodically.

- Web Address:

User Name:

Passwords:

- Web Address:

User Name:

Passwords:

- Web Address:

User Name:

Passwords:

- Web Address:

User Name:

Passwords:

- Web Address:

User Name:

Passwords:

Keep this book in a safe place. Date and change your passwords periodically.

R

- Web Address:
User Name:
Passwords:

- Web Address:
User Name:
Passwords:

- Web Address:
User Name:
Passwords:

- Web Address:
User Name:
Passwords:

- Web Address:
User Name:
Passwords:

Keep this book in a safe place. Date and change your passwords periodically.

- Web Address:
User Name:
Passwords:

- Web Address:
User Name:
Passwords:

- Web Address:
User Name:
Passwords:

- Web Address:
User Name:
Passwords:

- Web Address:
User Name:
Passwords:

Keep this book in a safe place. Date and change your passwords periodically.

R

- **Web Address:**

User Name:

Passwords:

- **Web Address:**

User Name:

Passwords:

- **Web Address:**

User Name:

Passwords:

- **Web Address:**

User Name:

Passwords:

- **Web Address:**

User Name:

Passwords:

• **Web Address:**
User Name:
Passwords:

• **Web Address:**
User Name:
Passwords:

• **Web Address:**
User Name:
Passwords:

• **Web Address:**
User Name:
Passwords:

• **Web Address:**
User Name:
Passwords:

Keep this book in a safe place. Date and change your passwords periodically.

S

- Web Address:

User Name:

Passwords:

- Web Address:

User Name:

Passwords:

- Web Address:

User Name:

Passwords:

- Web Address:

User Name:

Passwords:

- Web Address:

User Name:

Passwords:

- **Web Address:**
User Name:
Passwords:

- **Web Address:**
User Name:
Passwords:

- **Web Address:**
User Name:
Passwords:

- **Web Address:**
User Name:
Passwords:

- **Web Address:**
User Name:
Passwords:

Keep this book in a safe place. Date and change your passwords periodically.

S

- Web Address:
User Name:
Passwords:

- Web Address:
User Name:
Passwords:

- Web Address:
User Name:
Passwords:

- Web Address:
User Name:
Passwords:

- Web Address:
User Name:
Passwords:

- Web Address:
User Name:
Passwords:

- Web Address:
User Name:
Passwords:

- Web Address:
User Name:
Passwords:

- Web Address:
User Name:
Passwords:

- Web Address:
User Name:
Passwords:

Keep this book in a safe place. Date and change your passwords periodically.

S

- **Web Address:**

User Name:

Passwords:

- **Web Address:**

User Name:

Passwords:

- **Web Address:**

User Name:

Passwords:

- **Web Address:**

User Name:

Passwords:

- **Web Address:**

User Name:

Passwords:

- Web Address:

User Name:

Passwords:

- Web Address:

User Name:

Passwords:

- Web Address:

User Name:

Passwords:

- Web Address:

User Name:

Passwords:

- Web Address:

User Name:

Passwords:

Keep this book in a safe place. Date and change your passwords periodically.

T

- Web Address:

User Name:

Passwords:

- Web Address:

User Name:

Passwords:

- Web Address:

User Name:

Passwords:

- Web Address:

User Name:

Passwords:

- Web Address:

User Name:

Passwords:

- Web Address:
User Name:
Passwords:

- Web Address:
User Name:
Passwords:

- Web Address:
User Name:
Passwords:

- Web Address:
User Name:
Passwords:

- Web Address:
User Name:
Passwords:

Keep this book in a safe place. Date and change your passwords periodically.

T

- Web Address:

User Name:

Passwords:

- Web Address:

User Name:

Passwords:

- Web Address:

User Name:

Passwords:

- Web Address:

User Name:

Passwords:

- Web Address:

User Name:

Passwords:

Keep this book in a safe place. Date and change your passwords periodically.

- Web Address:
User Name:
Passwords:

- Web Address:
User Name:
Passwords:

- Web Address:
User Name:
Passwords:

- Web Address:
User Name:
Passwords:

- Web Address:
User Name:
Passwords:

Keep this book in a safe place. Date and change your passwords periodically.

T

- **Web Address:**____________________

User Name: ____________________

Passwords: ____________________

- **Web Address:**____________________

User Name: ____________________

Passwords: ____________________

- **Web Address:**____________________

User Name: ____________________

Passwords: ____________________

- **Web Address:**____________________

User Name: ____________________

Passwords: ____________________

- **Web Address:**____________________

User Name: ____________________

Passwords: ____________________

- Web Address:
User Name:
Passwords:

- Web Address:
User Name:
Passwords:

- Web Address:
User Name:
Passwords:

- Web Address:
User Name:
Passwords:

- Web Address:
User Name:
Passwords:

U

- Web Address: ______________________

User Name: ______________________

Passwords: ______________________

- Web Address: ______________________

User Name: ______________________

Passwords: ______________________

- Web Address: ______________________

User Name: ______________________

Passwords: ______________________

- Web Address: ______________________

User Name: ______________________

Passwords: ______________________

- Web Address: ______________________

User Name: ______________________

Passwords: ______________________

- Web Address:

User Name:

Passwords:

- Web Address:

User Name:

Passwords:

- Web Address:

User Name:

Passwords:

- Web Address:

User Name:

Passwords:

- Web Address:

User Name:

Passwords:

U

- Web Address:

User Name:

Passwords:

- Web Address:

User Name:

Passwords:

- Web Address:

User Name:

Passwords:

- Web Address:

User Name:

Passwords:

- Web Address:

User Name:

Passwords:

Keep this book in a safe place. Date and change your passwords periodically.

- Web Address:
User Name:
Passwords:

- Web Address:
User Name:
Passwords:

- Web Address:
User Name:
Passwords:

- Web Address:
User Name:
Passwords:

- Web Address:
User Name:
Passwords:

U

- **Web Address:** ____________________
User Name: ____________________
Passwords: ____________________

- **Web Address:** ____________________
User Name: ____________________
Passwords: ____________________

- **Web Address:** ____________________
User Name: ____________________
Passwords: ____________________

- **Web Address:** ____________________
User Name: ____________________
Passwords: ____________________

- **Web Address:** ____________________
User Name: ____________________
Passwords: ____________________

- Web Address:
User Name:
Passwords:

- Web Address:
User Name:
Passwords:

- Web Address:
User Name:
Passwords:

- Web Address:
User Name:
Passwords:

- Web Address:
User Name:
Passwords:

V

- **Web Address:**

User Name:

Passwords:

- **Web Address:**

User Name:

Passwords:

- **Web Address:**

User Name:

Passwords:

- **Web Address:**

User Name:

Passwords:

- **Web Address:**

User Name:

Passwords:

Keep this book in a safe place. Date and change your passwords periodically.

V

- **Web Address:**

User Name:

Passwords:

- **Web Address:**

User Name:

Passwords:

- **Web Address:**

User Name:

Passwords:

- **Web Address:**

User Name:

Passwords:

- **Web Address:**

User Name:

Passwords:

V

- Web Address:

User Name:

Passwords:

- Web Address:

User Name:

Passwords:

- Web Address:

User Name:

Passwords:

- Web Address:

User Name:

Passwords:

- Web Address:

User Name:

Passwords:

- **Web Address:** ______
User Name: ______
Passwords: ______

- **Web Address:** ______
User Name: ______
Passwords: ______

- **Web Address:** ______
User Name: ______
Passwords: ______

- **Web Address:** ______
User Name: ______
Passwords: ______

- **Web Address:** ______
User Name: ______
Passwords: ______

V

- **Web Address:**

User Name:

Passwords:

- **Web Address:**

User Name:

Passwords:

- **Web Address:**

User Name:

Passwords:

- **Web Address:**

User Name:

Passwords:

- **Web Address:**

User Name:

Passwords:

- **Web Address:**

User Name:

Passwords:

- **Web Address:**

User Name:

Passwords:

- **Web Address:**

User Name:

Passwords:

- **Web Address:**

User Name:

Passwords:

- **Web Address:**

User Name:

Passwords:

Keep this book in a safe place. Date and change your passwords periodically.

W

- Web Address: ___
User Name: ___
Passwords: ___

- Web Address: ___
User Name: ___
Passwords: ___

- Web Address: ___
User Name: ___
Passwords: ___

- Web Address: ___
User Name: ___
Passwords: ___

- Web Address: ___
User Name: ___
Passwords: ___

• Web Address:
User Name:
Passwords:

• Web Address:
User Name:
Passwords:

• Web Address:
User Name:
Passwords:

• Web Address:
User Name:
Passwords:

• Web Address:
User Name:
Passwords:

Keep this book in a safe place. Date and change your passwords periodically.

W

- Web Address:

User Name:

Passwords:

- Web Address:

User Name:

Passwords:

- Web Address:

User Name:

Passwords:

- Web Address:

User Name:

Passwords:

- Web Address:

User Name:

Passwords:

Keep this book in a safe place. Date and change your passwords periodically.

- Web Address:
User Name:
Passwords:

- Web Address:
User Name:
Passwords:

- Web Address:
User Name:
Passwords:

- Web Address:
User Name:
Passwords:

- Web Address:
User Name:
Passwords:

Keep this book in a safe place. Date and change your passwords periodically.

W

- Web Address:
User Name:
Passwords:

- Web Address:
User Name:
Passwords:

- Web Address:
User Name:
Passwords:

- Web Address:
User Name:
Passwords:

- Web Address:
User Name:
Passwords:

Keep this book in a safe place. Date and change your passwords periodically.

• Web Address: ______________________
User Name: ______________________
Passwords: ______________________

• Web Address: ______________________
User Name: ______________________
Passwords: ______________________

• Web Address: ______________________
User Name: ______________________
Passwords: ______________________

• Web Address: ______________________
User Name: ______________________
Passwords: ______________________

• Web Address: ______________________
User Name: ______________________
Passwords: ______________________

Keep this book in a safe place. Date and change your passwords periodically.

X

- Web Address:
User Name:
Passwords:

- Web Address:
User Name:
Passwords:

- Web Address:
User Name:
Passwords:

- Web Address:
User Name:
Passwords:

- Web Address:
User Name:
Passwords:

- Web Address:

User Name:

Passwords:

- Web Address:

User Name:

Passwords:

- Web Address:

User Name:

Passwords:

- Web Address:

User Name:

Passwords:

- Web Address:

User Name:

Passwords:

Keep this book in a safe place. Date and change your passwords periodically.

X

- Web Address:
User Name:
Passwords:

- Web Address:
User Name:
Passwords:

- Web Address:
User Name:
Passwords:

- Web Address:
User Name:
Passwords:

- Web Address:
User Name:
Passwords:

Keep this book in a safe place. Date and change your passwords periodically.

- Web Address:

User Name:

Passwords:

- Web Address:

User Name:

Passwords:

- Web Address:

User Name:

Passwords:

- Web Address:

User Name:

Passwords:

- Web Address:

User Name:

Passwords:

Keep this book in a safe place. Date and change your passwords periodically.

X

- Web Address:
User Name:
Passwords:

- Web Address:
User Name:
Passwords:

- Web Address:
User Name:
Passwords:

- Web Address:
User Name:
Passwords:

- Web Address:
User Name:
Passwords:

- Web Address:
User Name:
Passwords:

- Web Address:
User Name:
Passwords:

- Web Address:
User Name:
Passwords:

- Web Address:
User Name:
Passwords:

- Web Address:
User Name:
Passwords:

Keep this book in a safe place. Date and change your passwords periodically.

Y

- Web Address:
User Name:
Passwords:

- Web Address:
User Name:
Passwords:

- Web Address:
User Name:
Passwords:

- Web Address:
User Name:
Passwords:

- Web Address:
User Name:
Passwords:

Keep this book in a safe place. Date and change your passwords periodically.

- Web Address: ____________________
User Name: ____________________
Passwords: ____________________

- Web Address: ____________________
User Name: ____________________
Passwords: ____________________

- Web Address: ____________________
User Name: ____________________
Passwords: ____________________

- Web Address: ____________________
User Name: ____________________
Passwords: ____________________

- Web Address: ____________________
User Name: ____________________
Passwords: ____________________

Keep this book in a safe place. Date and change your passwords periodically.

Y

- **Web Address:**

User Name:

Passwords:

- **Web Address:**

User Name:

Passwords:

- **Web Address:**

User Name:

Passwords:

- **Web Address:**

User Name:

Passwords:

- **Web Address:**

User Name:

Passwords:

- Web Address:________________________________
User Name: ________________________________
Passwords: ________________________________

- Web Address:________________________________
User Name: ________________________________
Passwords: ________________________________

- Web Address:________________________________
User Name: ________________________________
Passwords: ________________________________

- Web Address:________________________________
User Name: ________________________________
Passwords: ________________________________

- Web Address:________________________________
User Name: ________________________________
Passwords: ________________________________

Y

- **Web Address:**
User Name:
Passwords:

- **Web Address:**
User Name:
Passwords:

- **Web Address:**
User Name:
Passwords:

- **Web Address:**
User Name:
Passwords:

- **Web Address:**
User Name:
Passwords:

- Web Address:

User Name:

Passwords:

- Web Address:

User Name:

Passwords:

- Web Address:

User Name:

Passwords:

- Web Address:

User Name:

Passwords:

- Web Address:

User Name:

Passwords:

Keep this book in a safe place. Date and change your passwords periodically.

Z

- **Web Address:**
User Name:
Passwords:

- **Web Address:**
User Name:
Passwords:

- **Web Address:**
User Name:
Passwords:

- **Web Address:**
User Name:
Passwords:

- **Web Address:**
User Name:
Passwords:

- Web Address:

User Name:

Passwords:

- Web Address:

User Name:

Passwords:

- Web Address:

User Name:

Passwords:

- Web Address:

User Name:

Passwords:

- Web Address:

User Name:

Passwords:

Z

- Web Address:

User Name:

Passwords:

- Web Address:

User Name:

Passwords:

- Web Address:

User Name:

Passwords:

- Web Address:

User Name:

Passwords:

- Web Address:

User Name:

Passwords:

Keep this book in a safe place. Date and change your passwords periodically.

- **Web Address:**
User Name:
Passwords:

- **Web Address:**
User Name:
Passwords:

- **Web Address:**
User Name:
Passwords:

- **Web Address:**
User Name:
Passwords:

- **Web Address:**
User Name:
Passwords:

Keep this book in a safe place. Date and change your passwords periodically.

NOTES:

Made in the USA
Monee, IL
04 November 2026

67376806R00089